Carl Czerny
1791 – 1857

100 easy Exercises
100 leichte Übungsstücke · 100 Exercices faciles

for Piano
für Klavier
pour Piano

opus 139

Edited by / Herausgegeben von / Edité par
Wilhelm Ohmen

ED 9821
ISMN 979-0-001-13813-0

www.schott-music.com

Mainz · London · Berlin · Madrid · New York · Paris · Prague · Tokyo · Toronto
© 2007 SCHOTT MUSIC GmbH & Co. KG, Mainz · Printed in Germany

Preface

Carl Czerny was born in Vienna on 20 February 1791 and lived there until his death on 15 July 1857, rarely leaving the city of his birth. His father was the respected piano teacher Wenzel Czerny, under whose instruction and influence Carl started playing the piano at the age of three; thanks to the boy's remarkable gifts and hard work, Ludwig van Beethoven took him on as a pupil when he was only nine. Carl Czerny performed Beethoven's works in public and later published them: these editions with their accompanying explanations, and in particular Czerny's writings *On the correct way to perform all Beethoven's piano works* (Universal Edition Vienna, UE 13340) have been a source of essential advice and inspiration for generations of pianists.

Czerny was a prolific composer who left behind him more than a thousand works. Besides his collections of studies, where a single opus number often represents fifty or more pieces, he also composed masses, operas, orchestral, piano and chamber music works in the early Romantic style. Igor Stravinsky speaks of *Czerny the red-blooded musician, whom he rated even higher as such than as an influential teacher*. Even as a young man, Czerny was recognised and much in demand as a piano teacher. He taught many pupils and trained a number of pianists, including Franz Liszt.

His major legacy, however, is the studies and tutorial works he wrote for the piano. It was Czerny's aim to give an outline presentation of all the figures and patterns of notes that pianists in his day were likely to encounter and to arrange them for tuition purposes. His collections of studies range from initial finger exercises for beginners to extensive and extremely difficult studies. *Hard work and plenty of practice are the only reliable paths to success*, according to Czerny. He also called for sensitive musical interpretation, though: *the beauty of playing and the sensitivity that approaches the simplicity of song*.

The pieces in this volume are intended for pianists at intermediate level. Very easy to begin with, with both hands playing in the treble clef until No. 15, they become progressively larger in scope and more demanding. The variety of technical devices in each piece makes them seem less like mere studies, while encouraging a fluent playing style and developing flexibility in the hand.

All the major and minor keys are included, as in other collections of pieces by Czerny. Numbers 87, 89, 90 and 92 offer a particularly charming and useful introduction to enharmonic changes (e.g. D♭ major / C♯ minor in No. 87). Czerny inserted a table of chords between Nos. 76 and 77 for cadences in every key, providing a useful guide for students learning to understand the cycle of fifths, with appropriate key signatures.

This set of pieces does not require playing in octaves, which makes it easier for smaller hands to manage. The editor's index of technical aspects gives a guide to the main content of each piece that will be useful for teaching purposes.

Fingerings are by the editor and have been adapted to suit modern pianos. Fingerings in brackets may be used as alternatives. All the exercises should be practised slowly at first and then at gradually increasing tempo. These appealing pieces provide very helpful preliminary exercises as preparation for learning works in the piano repertoire from easy to intermediate level.

Wilhelm Ohmen
Translation Julia Rushworth

Index of technical aspects

Vorwort

Carl Czerny wurde am 20. Februar 1791 in Wien als Sohn des geschätzten Klavierlehrers Wenzel Czerny geboren. Seine Heimatstadt verließ er nur selten und starb dort am 15. Juli 1857. Unterrichtet und geprägt von seinem Vater begann er schon im Alter von drei Jahren Klavier zu spielen und wurde dank seiner hohen Begabung, aber auch seines großen Fleißes wegen, im Alter von neun Jahren Schüler Ludwig van Beethovens. Dessen Werke spielte er öffentlich und gab sie später heraus. Für Generationen von Pianisten geben diese Ausgaben, seine überlieferten Erläuterungen, vor allem auch seine Schrift *Über den richtigen Vortrag der sämtlichen Beethoven'schen Klavierwerke* (Universal Edition Wien, UE 13340) wichtige Hinweise und Anregungen für deren Interpretation.

Czerny war ein leidenschaftlicher Komponist. Er schrieb mehr als eintausend Werke. Neben seinen Etüdensammlungen, bei denen eine Opuszahl oft aus fünfzig oder mehr Einzelstücken besteht, komponierte er Messen, Opern, Orchester-, Klavier- und kammermusikalische Werke in sensiblem frühromantischen Stil. Igor Strawinsky spricht vom *blutvollen Musiker Czerny, den er noch höher schätze als den bedeutenden Pädagogen.* Czerny war schon in jungen Jahren ein anerkannter und sehr gefragter Klavierpädagoge. Zahlreiche Klavierschüler und Pianisten bildete er aus, darunter auch Franz Liszt.

Bedeutend und unübersehbar aber sind sein Etüdenwerk und seine klaviermethodischen Schriften. Sein Ziel war es, alle möglichen, damals bekannten spieltechnischen Figuren und Bewegungsabläufe grundlegend darzustellen und für den Unterricht einzurichten. Seine Sammlungen reichen von den ersten Fingerübungen und Studien für den Anfänger bis hin zu ausgedehnten Etüden höchsten Schwierigkeitsgrades. *Fleiß und Übung sind die einzigen Garanten zum Erfolg –* so Czerny. Er fordert aber auch die sensible, einfühlsame musikalische Interpretation, die *Schönheit des Vortrags und Gefühls, welche dem einfachen Gesange zukommen.*

Die Stücke des vorliegenden Bandes sind für den etwas fortgeschrittenen Klavierspieler gedacht. Anfangs noch sehr leicht, bis Nr. 15 für beide Hände im Violinschlüssel notiert, werden sie zunehmend anspruchsvoller und umfangreicher. Durch verschiedenste technische Figuren innerhalb der Stücke wird ein Etüdencharakter vermieden. Eine flüssige Spielweise sowie Lockerung und Flexibilität der Hand werden gefördert.

Im Vergleich zu anderen Sammlungen Czernys werden alle Tonarten in Dur und Moll berücksichtigt. Die Stücke Nr. 87, 89, 90 und 92 sind mit ihren enharmonischen Vertauschungen (z. B. Des-Dur / Cis-Dur in Nr. 87) von besonderem Reiz und Nutzen. Zwischen Nr. 76 und 77 fügt Czerny eine Tabelle mit durch alle Tonarten kadenzierenden Dreiklängen ein, was zum Verständnis des Quintenzirkels mit den entsprechenden Vorzeichen für den Schüler sehr hilfreich sein wird.

In der Sammlung kommen keine Oktaven vor, was für die Bewältigung mit kleineren Händen vorteilhaft ist. Eine Übersicht des Herausgebers über die verschiedensten spieltechnischen Figuren und charakteristischen Inhalte wird für den Unterricht nützlich sein.

Die Fingersätze stammen vom Herausgeber und sind der Spielart auf heutigen Klavieren angepasst. Fingersätze in Klammern können alternativ angewendet werden. Alle Übungen sollen langsam einstudiert und im Tempo gesteigert werden. Die ansprechenden Stücke sind als Vorübungen für die Bewältigung der leichten bis mittelschweren Klavierliteratur sehr hilfreich.

Wilhelm Ohmen

Übersicht der spieltechnischen Themen

Albertische Begleitfiguren	Nr. 17, 23, 25, 29, 34, 94
Akkordbrechungen	Nr. 70, 71
Arpeggien	Nr. 46, 68
Cantable Stücke	Nr. 23, 47, 49, 51, 66, 73, 82, 93
Charakterstücke	Nr. 25, 31, 33, 48, 50, 55, 64, 76, 77, 82, 91
Chromatik	Nr. 32, 53
Enharmonische Vertauschung	Nr. 87, 89, 90, 92
Geläufigkeit	Nr. 19, 36, 37, 42, 61, 75, 77, 81, 83, 95, 100
Haltenoten	Nr. 43, 60, 77, 87
Handwechsel	Nr. 26, 97, 98, 99
Intervallbrechungen	Nr. 83, 86, 98
Märsche	Nr. 30, 52, 92
Phrasierung	Nr. 24, 27, 45, 59, 65, 81, 90
Polyphonie	Nr. 87
Punktierung	Nr. 8, 30, 41, 52, 62, 69, 72, 84, 94
Repetitionen	Nr. 27, 56, 57, 58, 96
Sexten	Nr. 7
Staccato	Nr. 24, 40, 46, 59, 65, 67, 80, 88, 96
Synkopen	Nr. 20, 44
Terzen	Nr. 11, 28, 38, 67, 90
Terzen (gebrochen)	Nr. 61
Terzen und Sexten	Nr. 16, 18
Triller	Nr. 34, 79, 85, 89
Triolen	Nr. 15, 57
Triolen gegen 8el	Nr. 54, 74
Triolen gegen 16tel	Nr. 54
Triolen in der Begleitung	Nr. 14, 22, 45, 62, 74, 78
Übergreifen der Hände	Nr. 22, 74, 99
Verzierungen	Nr. 23, 34, 39, 47, 49, 73, 93
Vorschläge	Nr. 12, 40

Contents / Inhalt

Part 1 / Teil 1

Part 2 / Teil 2

100 Exercises / 100 Übungsstücke

Part 1 / Teil 1

opus 139

Carl Czerny
1791 – 1857

Allegro moderato

20

Allegro, quasi presto

Marcia. Allegro maestoso

Allegretto vivo

Allegro

33

Andante espressivo

34

Allegro moderato

Allegro

p scherzando

40

Allegro molto

41

Allegro comodo

42

Allegro

Allegro molto

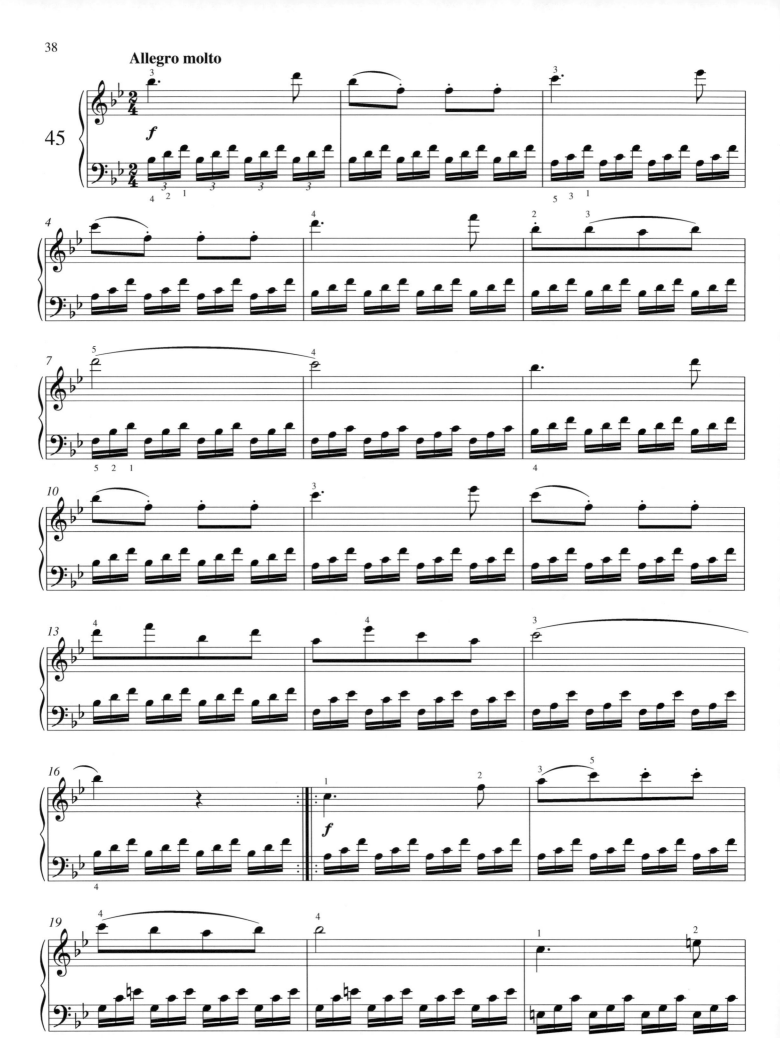

Moderato a la Marcia

Allegretto vivace

64

Lento cantabile

66

Andantino

67

Allegro vivo scherzando

71

Moderato quasi andantino

73

Allegro moderato

74

Allegro vivo ed energico

75

The pupil should play the following table from memory each day, indicating to the master the number of ♯ and ♭ demanded by the respective keys.

Folgende Tabelle hat der Schüler täglich auswendig zu spielen und dem Lehrer zu sagen, wie viele ♯ oder ♭ jede Tonart hat.

80

81

Allegretto moderato

82

Andante con moto ed espressivo

89

Andantino

90

Andante alla Marcia

Andantino grazioso ed espressivo

93

Allegretto

96

Allegro

98

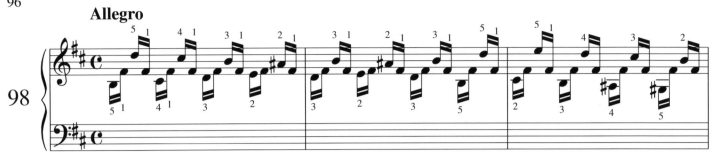

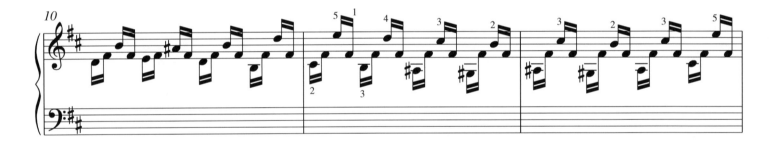

Allegro molto, quasi presto

99

Presto